**Discovering
Cultures**

Great Britain

Sharon Gordon

BENCHMARK BOOKS

MARSHALL CAVENDISH
NEW YORK

With thanks to Dr. Ruth Mitchell-Pitts, Associate Director, Center for European Studies, UNC–Chapel Hill, for the careful review of this manuscript.

Benchmark Books
Marshall Cavendish
99 White Plains Road
Tarrytown, New York 10591-9001
www.marshallcavendish.com

Library of Congress Cataloging-in-Publication Data

Gordon, Sharon.
Great Britain / by Sharon Gordon.
p. cm. — (Discovering cultures)
Summary: Highlights the geography, people, food, schools, recreation, celebrations, and language of Great Britain.
Includes bibliographical references and index.
ISBN 0-7614-1717-6
1. Great Britain — Juvenile literature. [1. Great Britain.] I. Title.
II. Series.
DA27.5.G6 2003
941—dc21   2003006956

Photo Research by Candlepants Incorporated

Front Cover Photo: Dallas and John Heaton/*Corbis*

The photographs in this book are used by permission and through the courtesy of; *Corbis*: Catherine Karnow, 1; Charles O'Rear, 4; Macduff Everton, 6; Wild Country, 7, 42 (left center); Jose Fusta Raga, 8, 43 (bottom right); Adam Woolfitt, 9; Bo Zaunders, 10; Annie Griffiths Belt, 11, 28; Pawel Libera, 12; Archivo Iconographica S.A., 13, 43 (top left); Sarah Jackson/Edifice, 14; Robert Estall, 16-17; Bill Ross, 18, 43 (top right); Martin Jones, 19; Niall Benvie, 20–21; John Heseltine, 22; Phillippa Lewis/Edifice, 24; Bryn Colton/Assignment Photographers, 25, 30, 43 (left center), back cover; Chris Andrews/ Chris Andrews Publications, 26; Martin B. Withers/Frank Lane Picture Agency, 29; Nigel Farrow/Assignments Photographers, 31, 43 (right center); Torleif Svensson, 32 (top); Michael Cole, 32 (lower); Michael Boys, 34 (left); Michael St. Muir Sheil, 34; Tim Graham, 35, 38; Robbie Jack, 36; Peter Turnley, 37 (top), 43 (bottom left); Yiorgos Nikiteas/Eye Ubiquitous, 37 (low); Bettmann, 39, 44 (right), 45; Tim Graham/Sygma, 44 (left).

Cover: *London's Tower Bridge*; Title page: *A Scottish farmer carries one of his sheep.*

Map and illustrations by Ian Warpole
Book design by Virginia Pope

Printed in China
1 3 5 6 4 2

Turn the Pages...

Where in the World Is Great Britain?

The island of Great Britain is on the western edge of Europe. It is 20 miles (32 kilometers) north of France. The English Channel separates Great Britain from France. The island is surrounded by the Irish Sea and the Atlantic Ocean on the west. The North Sea is on the east. Great Britain is made up of three different countries: England, Scotland, and Wales. Along with Northern Ireland, the four countries form the United Kingdom.

The coastline of Cornwall, England

Ben Nevis in Scotland is Britain's highest peak.

dyke is up to 20 feet (6 meters) high. A ditch runs along the Welsh side. It was built in the eighth century by King Offa to keep the Welsh out of England.

The river Tweed separates England from Scotland. The capital of Scotland is Edinburgh. The Scottish landscape is thick and green. Sheep are raised for wool in the Highlands. The highest point in Great Britain is found in Scotland. Ben Nevis (the mountain of snows) is 4,409 feet (1,344 m) high. It is near Loch Ness, the deepest lake in Scotland. The lake is the home of the Loch Ness Monster. This legendary creature made Loch Ness famous. People travel from all over the world hoping to see it.

England has a variety of landscapes. Near the Scottish border, there are highlands and mountains. In the south and central areas, there are rolling hills and green fields. This area has good soil for growing wheat, barley, and potatoes. Dairy farms produce delicious cheese and milk. The fields provide good grazing lands for cattle.

London is the capital of England. It is the largest city in Europe, with about seven million people. The river Thames divides London in two. On the east are many important places, including Westminster Palace. The British Parliament, which is like the U.S. Congress, meets here to make laws. On top of Westminster is the famous clock tower. Its bell, called Big Ben, weighs more than 26,000 pounds (11,793 kilograms). The famous Piccadilly Circus is on the west side of the Thames. Piccadilly Circus is not really a circus. It is an open area filled with restaurants, shops, museums, and theaters.

The town of Plymouth is an old seaport in southwest England. The harbor is always busy with ships coming and going. One of the most famous ships to leave Plymouth Harbor was the *Mayflower*. It carried the Pilgrims on their historic voyage to America in 1620.

Visitors to London enjoy seeing Big Ben's famous clock tower.

Shetland Ponies

These little horses are only three feet (1 m) high! They come from the Shetland Islands, which are 100 miles (161 km) north of Scotland. Shetland ponies were once used to pull loads of coal out of mines. Their size helped them get into the small mine *shafts*. Their great strength helped them pull the heavy loads. Today, Shetland ponies are used as pets. They are perfect for teaching children how to ride a horse.

What Makes Great Britain British?

The word "British" is used to describe all the people of Great Britain. People from England are "English." Those from Scotland are "Scots" and those from Wales are "Welsh." Like the United States, people from many continents live in Great Britain. Some came from countries in Asia, Africa, and the West Indies that were once ruled by Britain.

Scottish boy playing the bagpipes

Children from many countries live in Great Britain.

Most British people belong to the Church of England, or the Anglican Church. Many belong to the Roman Catholic, Methodist, or Baptist churches. Some are Jewish. Others are Muslims. Many people who have come to Great Britain from India also follow the Hindu or Sikh religions.

The royal family is an important part of British history. The royal family's home is at Buckingham Palace in London. The king or queen of England is the head of the royal family and of Great Britain. Since 1952, England's queen has been

Buckingham Palace is the home of the royal family.

Queen Elizabeth II. Her son, Prince Charles, is the prince of Wales. When the queen dies, or leaves the throne, Charles will become the next king.

The prime minister is in charge of the British government. The British Parliament makes laws. The Parliament is made up of the House of Commons, the House of Lords, and the queen. The House of Commons has the most power. The British people vote for the members of the House of Commons in an election. The people do not vote for the members of the House of Lords. Their positions are passed on within families. The countries within the United Kingdom also vote for leaders of their local governments.

English is the official language of Great Britain. The English language is spoken all over the world. It was first used in Great Britain, and spread quickly to other nations. It came to America with the early settlers. Today, schoolchildren in many countries learn English.

Although most people speak English in Great Britain, other languages are also spoken. In Wales, an old Celtic language is spoken by some of the Welsh. A Scottish Gaelic is spoken in parts of Scotland.

The British love good music. Every year since 1895, the Promenade Concerts, or Proms, are held in London. The word "promenade" means to walk around. That is exactly what the audience used to do during these concerts. The Proms include classical, jazz, and other styles of music. They take place from July to September.

Great Britain has given the world some of the finest writers and poets. England's William Shakespeare wrote many famous plays, including *Romeo and Juliet*. Mary Shelley was born in London. She wrote *Frankenstein* when she was only twenty-one. Robert Burns was a Scottish poet. New Year's Eve parties would not be complete without singing his famous song "Auld Lang Syne."

Great Britain is known for its historic buildings and architecture. Some of the

The Salisbury Cathedral has the tallest spire in all of Great Britain.

best examples can be found in its oldest cathedrals. They are known for their tall church *spires* and roomy interiors. The cathedral at Salisbury, built in 1258, has the tallest spire in Great Britain. It is 404 feet (123 m) high.

The English cottage is a common sight in the country. Many cottages have thatched roofs. Thatching is an old British craft in which reeds are laid together to make a roof. In northern England and Scotland, *heather* is sometimes used as thatch material. When the railroads were built, hard materials like *slate* could be shipped for roofing. For a while, thatched roofs became less popular and were a sign of being poor. But today, cottages with thatched roofs are very valuable. Their owners take good care of them.

To many British families, a thatched-roof cottage is home, sweet home.

Stonehenge

An ancient structure called Stonehenge can be found in southern England. It is believed to be five thousand years old. Stonehenge means "the hanging stones." The carefully placed stones form a 100-foot (30-m) circle. Each stone weighs about 90,000 pounds (40,823 kg). No one knows how these huge stones were brought from South Wales and moved into place. It would take 600 people to move one stone more than half an inch! Scientists think that ancient people used Stonehenge to tell the seasons of the year. Others think it might have been part of a religious ceremony.

No one knows for sure.

Living in Great Britain

More than 80 percent of British people live in houses or cottages. The rest live in flats, or apartments, in the big cities. British homes are often made of concrete or brick because of the damp weather. A typical house has five or six rooms.

The workday usually begins at 8 or 9 A.M. Most people work five days a week. Each year, they get two or three weeks holiday, or vacation. Those with more education and better jobs usually get more vacation time.

Most people own their own cars, although they often use public transportation to get to work. People drive on the left side of the road in Great Britain. The steering wheel is on the right.

The Channel Tunnel, or Chunnel, was built under the English Channel in 1994. It is 31

Homes in a London suburb

miles (50 km) long and connects England and France. Trains zip through the tunnel in about 35 minutes. The Chunnel has helped link residents of Great Britain to the rest of Europe. Some people use it to travel to work. The Chunnel also helps families get to the southern, warmer areas of Europe for vacation.

After World War II, many people left Britain's big cities

This modern train speeds through the Channel Tunnel.

Colorful flowers bloom in window boxes across Great Britain.

and moved to the suburbs. They travel to work in the city each day. Many housing developments were built in the suburbs. But there are not enough homes close to the cities. In some areas, old factories are being turned into loft apartments. This allows more people to live closer to work.

Many families in Great Britain love gardening. Towns often rent people small patches of land for gardening. Some city people keep a garden in the country. The wet weather is perfect for growing beautiful flowers and shrubs. The warmer

temperatures allow flowers to bloom in February. Bright red geraniums grow in window boxes in the city. Purple heather covers the countryside.

Meals are simple in Great Britain. Breakfast might be cereal or tea and toast. On weekends, eggs and sausage or bacon with baked beans might be served. The most common take-out meal is fish 'n' chips. The chips are large fried

Fish 'n' chips are a favorite take-out food.

Fields of beautiful heather grow in the Scottish Highlands.

potatoes, like french fries, served with a piece of fried fish. British dinners are usually a piece of meat that is boiled or roasted. It may be served with vegetables, bread, and a dessert.

If it is 4 P.M. in Britain, it must be teatime. Often, tea is served with a snack, like a cake or biscuit. Wealthy families sip tea from fine china cups. Tea came to Great Britain from China in the mid-seventeenth century. Today, Britain is filled with places to get a good "cuppa" tea. Coffee shops are also popular.

The British love their afternoon tea.

Let's Eat!
Toad in the Hole

This is a favorite of children in Great Britain. Ask an adult to help you prepare this recipe. You can use pork, beef, or vegetarian sausages. Soy milk can be used instead of cow's milk.

Ingredients:

1 pound thin sausage

$3/4$ cup flour

$1/2$ teaspoon salt

$3/4$ cup milk

1 tablespoon water

2 large eggs

Wash your hands. Preheat the oven to 450 degrees Fahrenheit (232 degrees Celsius). Sift together the flour and salt. Add the milk and water and mix well.

In a separate bowl, beat the eggs until they are fluffy, but not stiff. Add the beaten eggs to the flour mixture. Beat with a whisk or electric mixer until bubbles rise to the surface of the batter. Refrigerate for 30 minutes.

Fry the sausages in a pan until they are well browned. Spoon about 2 or 3 tablespoons of the fat from the sausages into a medium-sized baking dish. Then place the sausages into the dish and pour the batter over them.

Bake for 10 minutes. Without opening the oven, reduce the heat to 350 degrees Fahrenheit (177 degrees Celsius). Continue cooking for another 15 minutes, or until the batter has risen and is golden brown. Serves four.

School Days

Education is very important to the British. Families work hard to send their children to good schools. They want them to get good jobs and to have a comfortable life.

All children in Great Britain must start school at the age of five. They must stay in school until the age of sixteen. Most children wear uniforms to school. They go to school from 8 or 8:30 A.M. to 3:30 P.M., with an hour for lunch. After school, they might play football or netball. These are the British names for soccer and basketball.

From age five to twelve, children go to primary school. They go to secondary school from age twelve to sixteen. England and Wales have similar school systems. Children study English, math, science, technology, music, art, and physical education.

On the playground in England

Most students go to a state school.

They take special tests every few years to check their progress. At sixteen, they take tests known as the General Certificate of Secondary Education.

In Scotland, students wear uniforms that include a school badge and tie. Classes are small. At age sixteen, they receive a Scottish Certificate of Education. Scotland's school system is excellent. Scots like to say that their children do better on tests than English students.

Most British students go to schools that are paid for by the government. In Britain they are called state schools. Britain's public schools are not free. These schools would be called private schools in the United States. Sometimes children live away, or board, at these schools. Many of Britain's leaders have been educated at the best boarding schools.

Some children who are blind or deaf might go to state schools. Others go to special boarding schools. Great Britain also has many schools for students with different learning needs.

Oxford University college buildings in the winter

Around 50 percent of students in Great Britain continue their education after secondary school. Welsh students can study at the University of Wales, which has seven campuses around the country. The University of St. Andrews is the oldest Scottish university. Oxford and Cambridge Universities in England are some of the oldest in the world. Women were not allowed to attend these universities until the middle of the 1800s. They could not earn a degree from Oxford until 1920.

Even before public education became a national right, the British liked reading. People kept books in their homes or borrowed them from libraries. They studied different subjects on their own. Sunday schools encouraged children to read the Bible.

Nursery Rhymes

Many nursery rhymes, such as *Jack & Jill* and *Humpty Dumpty*, are based on British history. The rhymes often made fun of the rich and famous without using their names. That way, the author would not get in trouble. It is said that *Dr. Foster* is about King Edward I of England. He traveled to the town of Gloucester (pronounced glos-ter) in the middle of a rainstorm. He and his horse fell into a large mud puddle. The people had to pull them out with wooden planks. The embarrassed king never returned to the town.

Dr. Foster

Dr. Foster went to Gloucester

In a shower of rain

He stepped in a puddle

Right up to his middle

And never went there again.

Just for Fun

Many British families like to relax by taking long walks. Britain's beautiful national parks and nature trails are popular. People can go hiking, climbing, fishing, or boating.

Hikers enjoy Great Britain's beautiful countryside.

Picnics are also a favorite outdoor activity. Fresh bread, cheese, and jam are common items in a British picnic basket.

British adults and children like to read books and watch the "telly," or television. In the evening, listening to the radio is almost as popular. British radio has programs and weekly shows, just like the television. The British Broadcasting Corporation (BBC) produces many fine radio and television shows. Some are available in the United States.

The British like keeping pets. Many families have either a dog, cat, or bird. Families also enjoy fixing up their homes in their spare time. Do-it-yourself television shows and books are very popular.

When it comes to sports, rugby is enjoyed throughout Great Britain. The Welsh especially love this game. It is similar to football as played in the United States. Rugby players can pass the oval ball to the side or backward, kick

British families take good care of their pets.

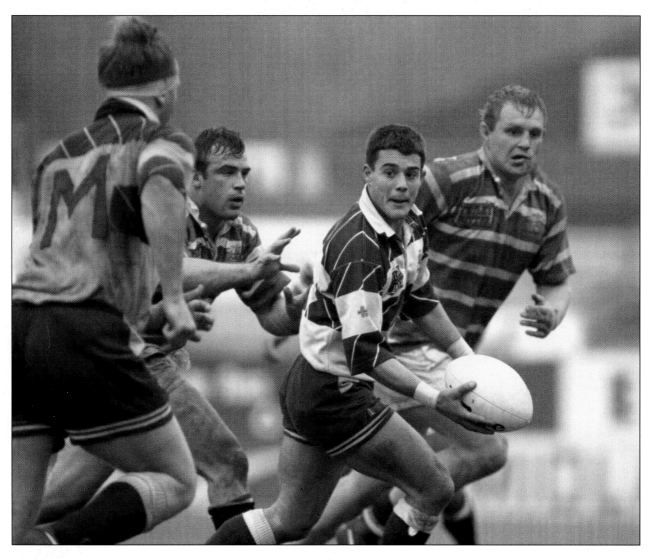

Athletes must be tough to play rugby.

it forward, or carry it to the goal. Huddles are called scrums. Although the players must tackle each other, they do not wear helmets or pads. They often get very bruised.

Another favorite British sport is cricket. It is played with a bat and ball. The game, which is more than 700 years old, is very difficult to learn. It has many complicated rules. It is also played in countries that were once British colonies, such as India, South Africa, and the West Indies. One cricket match can last several days.

Lawn bowling, or "bowls," is not like bowling in the United States. It is played outside on the grass. The first bowler rolls his ball, or jack, out onto the lawn. The other players try to come as close as they can to the first ball. Lawn-bowling clubs are popular throughout Great Britain.

Cricket is a favorite British sport.

The first golf game was played in Scotland.

The game of golf was invented in Scotland in the twelfth century. It is now a sport that is loved around the world, including the United States. Tennis is another favorite British sport. Each year, the best players around the world come to Wimbledon, near London. It is the only championship tennis game that is played on grass courts.

A junior tennis player at Wimbledon

Rounders

Rounders is a popular playground game in Britain. It is like baseball in the United States. Players strike a hard leather ball—the size of a tennis ball—with a wooden bat that is shorter than a baseball bat. Then they try to run around four bases—making a rounder—before the ball is returned to the pitcher. If a player cannot finish the round, he or she must stop at one of the bases and wait until the next player hits the ball.

Let's Celebrate!

People in Great Britain love to celebrate Christmas. They decorate their homes with lights and trees. They have friends and family over for a dinner of roast turkey, goose, or beef. Dessert might be a sweet *mince* pie or a Christmas pudding or cake. Families exchange gifts and cards. Many attend services at one of the Christian churches, such as the Anglican Church.

A table covered with holiday treats

London's Trafalgar Square decorated for Christmas

The queen's birthday is in April, but it is publicly celebrated in June. The British army marches in a parade called Trooping the Colour. Each *regiment* carries its own colorful flag. The queen views her troops while sitting in a horse-drawn carriage. Cannons are fired from the Tower of London.

The Edinburgh Festival in Scotland is held every August and lasts for two weeks. It is one of the world's most important cultural festivals. The festival attracts thousands of visitors from around the world. There are performances in dance, theater, and especially music. Groups perform rock, classical, folk, jazz, and opera. The highlight of

Queen Elizabeth II at
Trooping the Colour

Performers at the Edinburgh Festival

the fair is the Edinburgh Military Tattoo, a marching band of drums and Scottish bagpipes. The group marches in perfect order as they sing the Scottish favorite, "Scotland the Brave."

During a Scottish celebration, the men wear *kilts*. It is thought that the kilt originally came from the Scottish Highlands. Kilts are made from *tartans*, a type of plaid wool fabric. They identify what clan, or family, a person is from. Today's kilts are

Men wearing traditional Scottish kilts

thick and warm. A groom might wear a kilt at his wedding. Army units wear kilts for dress. In the front of the kilt hangs a *sporran*, a leather pouch for carrying things.

Each year, the British celebrate Guy Fawkes Day on November 5. On that day in 1605, a secret plan to kill King James I and the members of the Parliament was discovered. It was called the Gunpowder Plot. A group of men, including Guy Fawkes, had planned to light gunpowder in the basement of Parliament. Instead, they were caught and killed. To celebrate, some children make stuffed dummies named "Guys." They go into the streets to ask for "a penny for the Guy." They use the money to buy fireworks. At night, all the dummies are thrown in a pile and burned. The celebration continues with fireworks.

Children celebrate Guy Fawkes Day with sparklers.

Welsh girls celebrate St. David's Day in their traditional costumes.

On special occasions in Wales, women and children put on the Welsh national folk costume. They wear tall black hats and red cloaks and shawls. This costume was based on the clothing of Welsh women in the nineteenth century. Pictures of the costume were painted by local artists and sold as prints to tourists. The costume is worn on holidays such as Saint David's Day, on March 1. Saint David is the *patron saint* of Wales.

New Year's Eve is an important holiday in Scotland. People celebrate by going "first footing," or visiting their friends door-to-door. The "first foot" is the first person to step into your house after midnight, in the new year. With luck, that person will bring something good to eat or drink!

Christmas Cards

The tradition of sending Christmas cards to friends and relatives began in Great Britain in 1843. Henry Cole, a friend of the royal family, asked an artist to create a special Christmas greeting card. John Calcott Horsley made a card showing a family raising their glasses in a toast to faraway friends. One thousand copies were printed and mailed. The leftovers were sold to the public. A new Christmas tradition was born.

The British flag is called the Union Jack. It is the flag of the United Kingdom, which includes the three countries of Great Britain, as well as Northern Ireland. It combines the flags of the patron saints from each country. It is blue, with the red flag of Saint George for England, the diagonal white cross for Saint Andrew of Scotland, and the red diagonal cross of Ireland's Saint Patrick. Wales is not represented. This is because when the flag first appeared, Wales was already united with England.

The main unit of British money is the pound. There are one hundred pence in one pound. There are many coins for different amounts of pence, like the ten-pence coin shown here. There is also a one-pound coin and a two-pound coin. Scottish and Welsh coins have symbols from their own countries. Pounds come in paper bills, too. The exchange rate changes, but in 2003 one British pound equaled $1.58 in the United States.

Count in Welsh

English	Welsh	Say it like this:
one	un	een
two	dau	die
three	tri	tree
four	pedwar	ped-ooar
five	pump	pimp
six	chwech	k'ware'k
seven	saith	sigh'th
eight	wyth	oo-ith
nine	naw	naaw
ten	deg	dairg

Glossary

heather Low-growing plant with tiny purple flowers.

kilt Traditional Scottish plaid skirt for men.

mince Chopped mixture of raisins, apples, spices, and sometimes meat.

patron saint Saint who is believed to watch over a country.

regiment (reh-juh-ment) Unit of soldiers.

shaft Long narrow opening dug into the earth.

slate Hard rock that can be split into thin layers for roofing.

spire Tall and pointy part of a roof.

sporran Leather pouch that hangs in front of a kilt.

tartan A plaid woolen fabric used to make kilts.

Fast Facts

The main unit of British money is the pound.

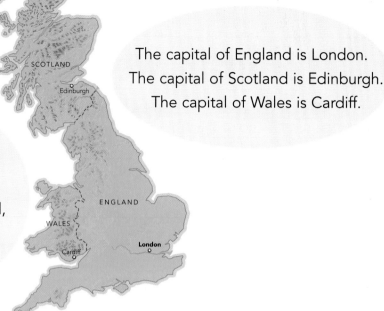

The island of Great Britain is made up of three countries: England, Scotland, and Wales.

The capital of England is London. The capital of Scotland is Edinburgh. The capital of Wales is Cardiff.

The British Parliament makes laws. The Parliament is made up of the House of Commons, the House of Lords, and the queen.

The prime minister is in charge of the British government.

Ben Nevis is Great Britain's tallest mountain. It is 4,409 feet (1,344 m) high.

The British flag is called the Union Jack.

The average rainfall in Great Britain is 40 inches (102 cm) per year.

The Channel Tunnel, or Chunnel, was built under the English Channel. It is 31 miles (50 km) long and connects England and France.

In 2003, in the United Kingdom, 40 million people were Anglican or Roman Catholic, 1.5 million were Muslim, 1 million were Sikh or Hindu, 760,000 were Methodist, and 350,000 were Jewish.

Rugby and cricket are popular British sports.

During a Scottish celebration, men wear skirts called kilts.

The London clock tower's famous bell, Big Ben, weighs more than 26,000 pounds (11,793 kg).

Proud to Be British

Florence Nightingale (1820–1910)

Florence Nightingale was taught at home in England by her father at a time when most girls did not get a good education. She became interested in social work and visited the sick in local villages. She wanted to become a nurse, but her parents wanted her to get married. In those days, it was not proper for an educated woman to be a nurse. In 1850, Nightingale went to Germany to study nursing. She went to Turkey during the Crimean War to help in the military hospitals. She quickly improved the conditions and was dearly loved by the soldiers. In 1860, she began the Nightingale Training School for nurses. Florence Nightingale brought respect to women in the nursing profession. In 1989, the Florence Nightingale Museum opened in London. Many of her books, letters, and nursing materials are on display.

J. K. Rowling (1965–)

Joanne Kathleen Rowling is a resident of Edinburgh, Scotland. She is the author of the popular *Harry Potter* books. Rowling grew up in Wales and went to the University of Exeter in England. She worked for Amnesty International in London on human rights issues. It was on a long train ride in England that she first thought of the characters for her Harry Potter books. She often wrote sitting in a coffee shop while her young daughter slept in her baby carriage. J. K. Rowling has won many children's book awards. Her stories have sold millions of copies both in Great Britain and the United States. They have been translated into twenty-eight languages.

John Wesley (1703–1791)

John Wesley was born in Lincolnshire, England. He is the founder of the Methodist church. In 1709, John was rescued from a late-night house fire. His mother felt he had been saved for a purpose. At Oxford, he met with a group called the Holy Club. Their strict "methods" of prayer and study gave them the name Methodists. In 1738, Wesley became a minister. He traveled thousands of miles to preach to crowds throughout Britain. The year 2003 marked the three hundredth anniversary of John Wesley's birth. Special events throughout Great Britain celebrated this church leader's life and work.

Find Out More

Books

Enchantment of the World: England by Jean F. Blashfield. Children's Press, Connecticut, 1997.

Enchantment of the World: Scotland by R. Conrad Stein. Children's Press, Connecticut, 2001.

Nations of the World: United Kingdom by Brian Innes. Raintree Steck-Vaughn Publishers, Texas, 2002.

Cultures of the World: Wales by Anna Hestler. Marshall Cavendish, New York, 2001.

Welcome to My Country: Welcome to England by Maree Lister, Marti Sevier, Roseline Ngcheong-Lum. Gareth Stevens Publishing, Wisconsin, 1999.

Web Sites

Visit the official Web site of Britain's royal family at **www.royal.gov.uk**.

Learn how to speak Welsh at **www.acen.co.uk/welshinaweek/how-to/**.

Go to **www.historic-scotland.gov.uk** to explore Scotland's historic architecture and ancient monuments.

Video

The British Isles Collection (3 video set), Questar Videos, 1992.

Index

Page numbers for illustrations are in **boldface.**

About the Author

Sharon Gordon has written many nature and science books for young children. She has worked as an advertising copywriter and a book club editor. She is writing other books for the *Discovering Cultures* series. Sharon and her husband Bruce have three teenage children, Douglas, Katie, and Laura, and one spoiled pooch, Samantha. They live in Midland Park, New Jersey. The family especially enjoys traveling to the Outer Banks of North Carolina. After she puts her three children through college, Sharon hopes to visit the many exciting places she has come to love through her writing and research.